GROOVIN' RUDIMENTS

I0811944

by Ron Wilson

Online Audio

To access the online audio recording go to:
WWW.MELBAY.COM/31024MEB

MEL BAY®

WWW.MELBAY.COM

About this Book

As a teacher and professional drummer, I am a firm believer in developing technique. Once beginning students learn some basic beats the question becomes, "How do you get to the next level?" I have found that developing the use of drum rudiments opens up a new universe. By working on the rudiments alone, the drummer builds technique, learns new sticking patterns and acquires speed and dexterity. When applying these patterns to the drum set in a groove or beat, these abilities create another dimension. Applying these techniques in a musical situation is the final step.

Don't forget about the music! An important part of this process is to apply it while playing with other instruments. The music tracks that accompany this book greatly enhance the learning process, make it more fun to play and will give you examples of how to use these concepts in a musical setting.

Each musical example includes two separate versions. One includes drums as a reference; the other leaves the drum tracks out, so the student can provide the drum part on their own. The music accompanying this book was written, produced and performed by Ron Wilson. Special thanks to Michael Wilson for adding his brilliant electric guitar playing.

Acknowledgements

I would like to thank Mara for her encouragement and support along with my sons RonLuc and Matthew. I must also thank my parents who endured years of loud practicing in the house and were always supportive of my musical pursuits. I owe them a debt of gratitude. Thanks also to Michael Wilson, Jeff Wilson, John Wilson, Lou Christie, Dan Haskins, Bruce Sheffler, Joe Hurtado, Horacee Arnold, Rick Barbour, Ray DesRoches and the countless musicians who have inspired me over the years.
For further information visit www.ronwilson.net.

Introduction

Greetings! This book was created to make the process of learning and practicing drum rudiments musical, enjoyable and practical. After years of working with drum students, I found myself being asked many of the same questions: Why should I learn this? Will I ever use this material when playing with a band? Learning rudiments is boring – can't we just learn rock tunes? So to answer those questions – I happen to believe that learning the rudiments of drumming is an important step and a valuable tool to becoming the musician you want to be. If the rudiments in this book are learned to a proficient level, you will find many uses for this material that will lead to a creative approach to playing most rhythms.

This book is intended to show how rudiments can be used in various musical settings. So, while it is important to take some time to learn each rudiment slowly at first, you can begin using the rudiments in musical situations almost immediately, which should provide an enjoyable outlet. I have included original music composed specifically to accompany the exercises in this book.

Each page introduces a new rudiment. The first line provides the rudiment alone. I recommend working on the rudiment on the snare drum or drum pad at first, without the drum set permutations. This will give you a solid foundation to then expand upon. The next step is to apply the rudiment as a drum set groove. Then, we apply the rudiment as a written fill. Bars that are marked as "Fill" give you an opportunity to create your own fills, using the pertinent rudiment in any fashion you like. It is important to follow the written accented notes. When the rhythms are played "straight", they can sometimes sound stiff. Use of the accents in the proper spots will help to make the rhythms feel better and create a deeper pocket or groove. Remember, the job of any musician is to not only play the proper notes, but also make the music "feel" good.

Most of the material in this book is written for three way coordination (snare, bass and hat). Once the drum set patterns are mastered as written, it may be beneficial to add the fourth limb. I would suggest playing the written hi-hat parts on the ride cymbal, and adding the hi-hat with your foot on beats 2 and 4 (or beat four if you are playing in 6/8 time) to the drum set grooves.

Above all, have fun!

Ron Wilson

Contents

Drum Set Notation Key

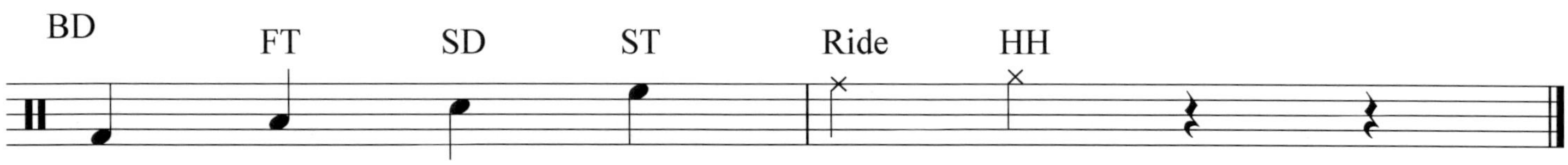

BD - Bass Drum

FT - Floor Tom

SD - Snare Drum

ST - Small Tom

Ride - Ride Cymbal

HH - Hi-Hat

Single Stroke Roll

Snare Drum

Groove

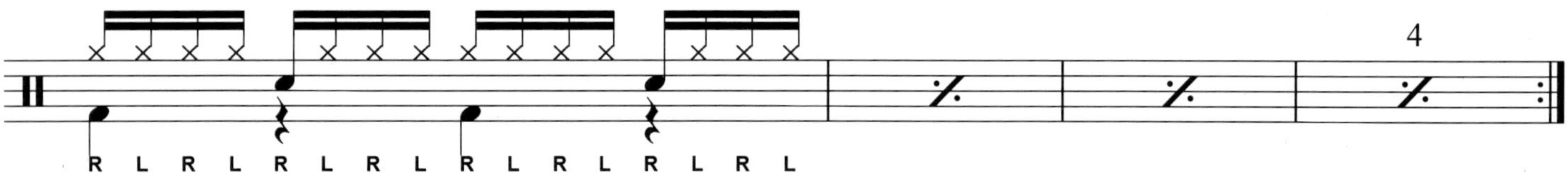

Play along with the music track "Funk": 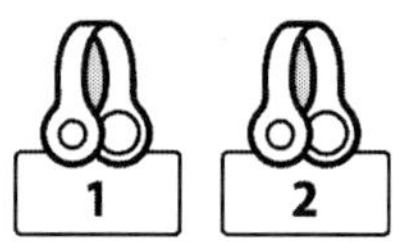

Fill

Open Fills

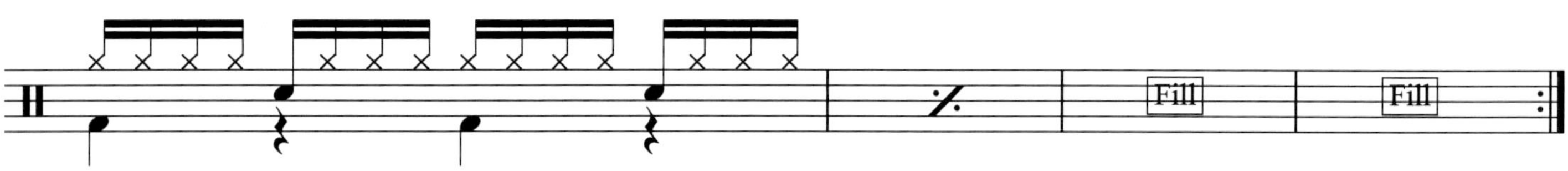

Single Stroke Four

Snare Drum

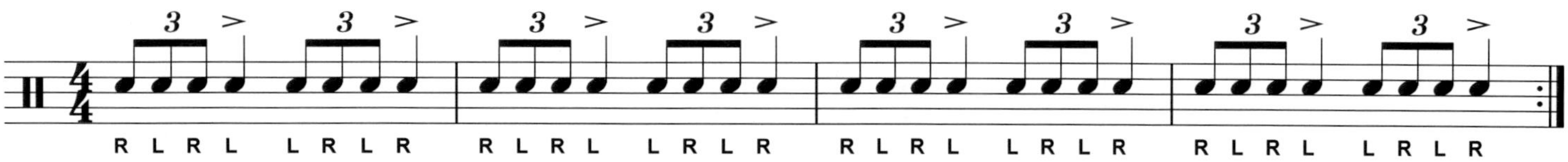

Groove

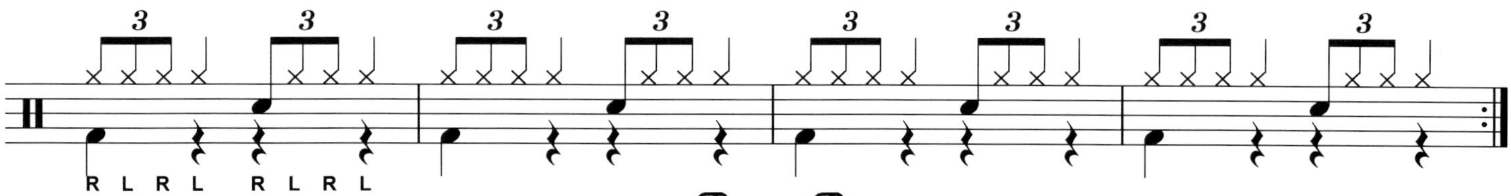

Play along to the music track "Buckshot": 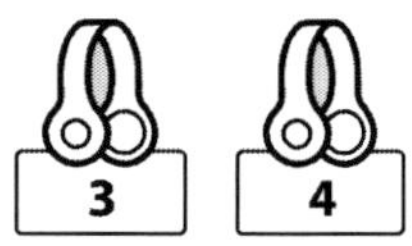

Fill

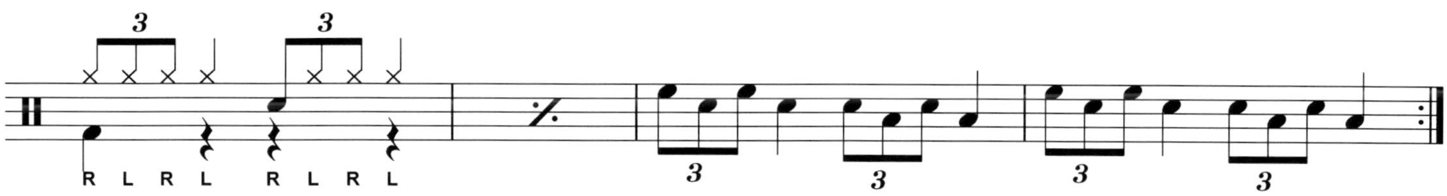

Open Fill

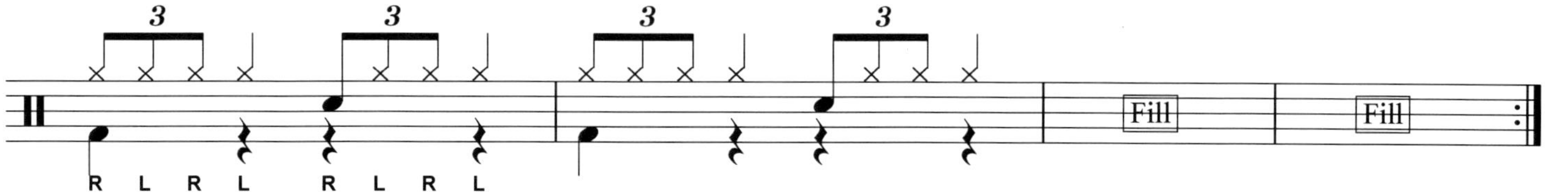

A slight variation creates a Bolero rhythm.

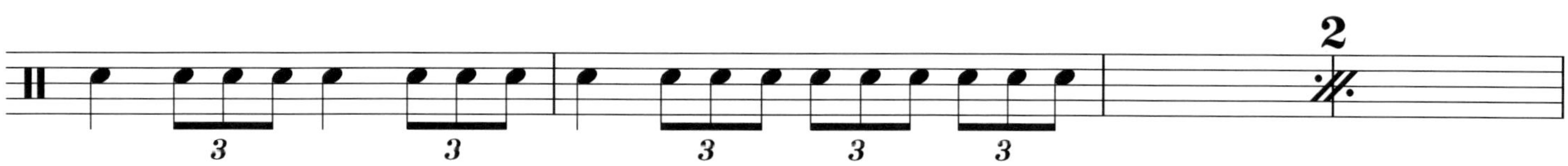

Single Stroke Seven

Snare Drum

Groove

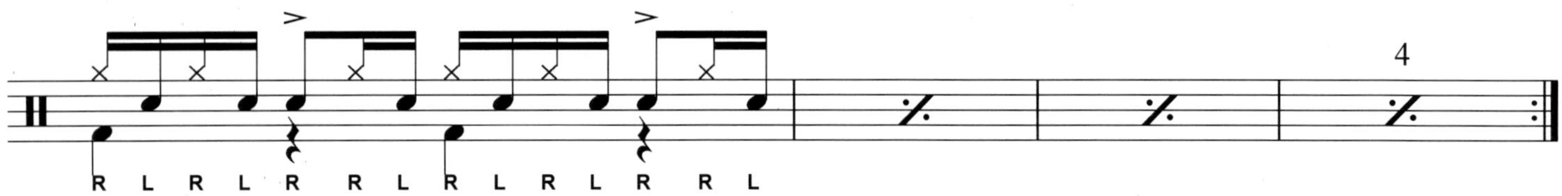

Fill

Play along to the music track "Funk": 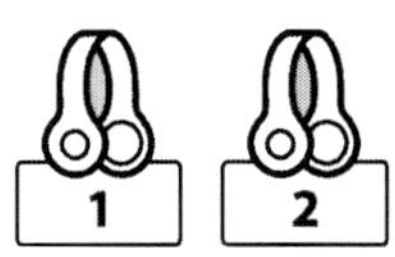

Open Fill

Buzz Roll

Snare Drum

A "buzz" is created by pressing down on the drum head with the bead of the stick and letting it bounce slightly.

Groove

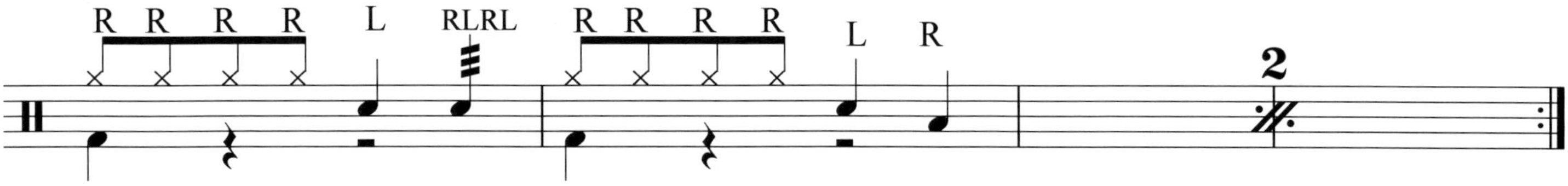

Fill

Play along to the music track "Half Time": 5 6

Open Fills

Triple Stroke

Snare Drum

Groove

Fill

Play along to music track "Slow Blues": 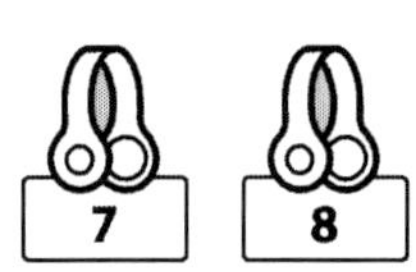

Open Fills

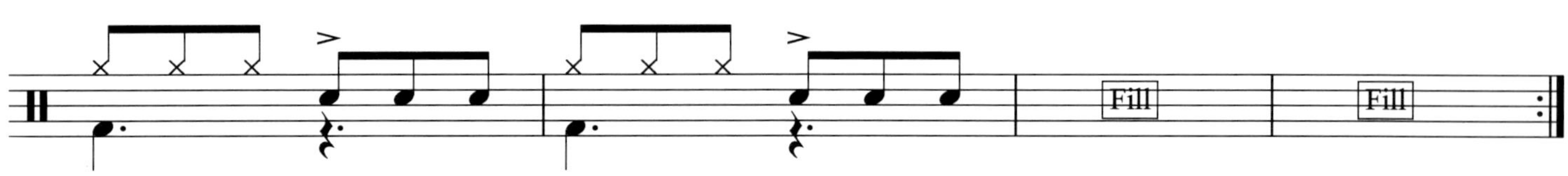

Double Stroke Roll

Snare Drum

Groove

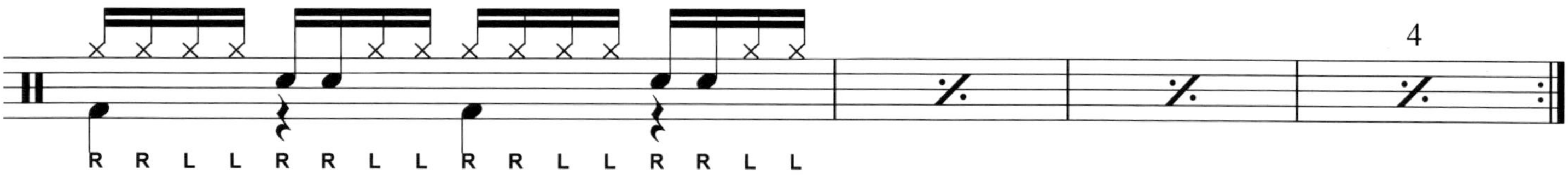

Fill

Play along to the music track "Funk":

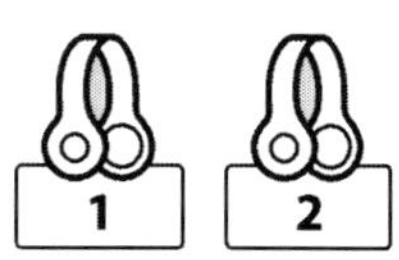

Open Fills

5 Stroke Roll

Snare Drum

Groove

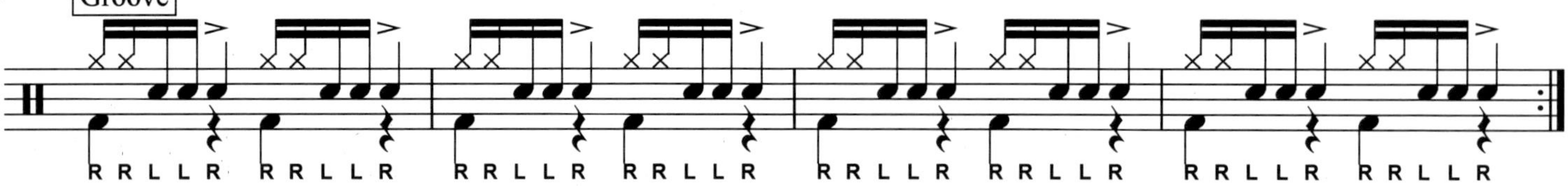

Fill #1

Play along to the music track "Aliens": 9 10 or "Funk": 1 2

Fill #2

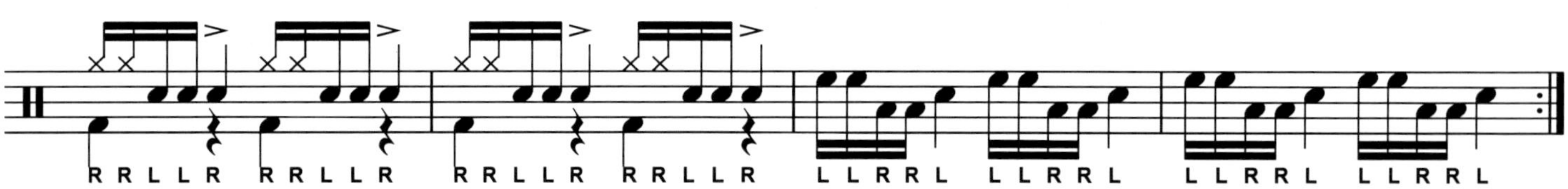

Open Fills

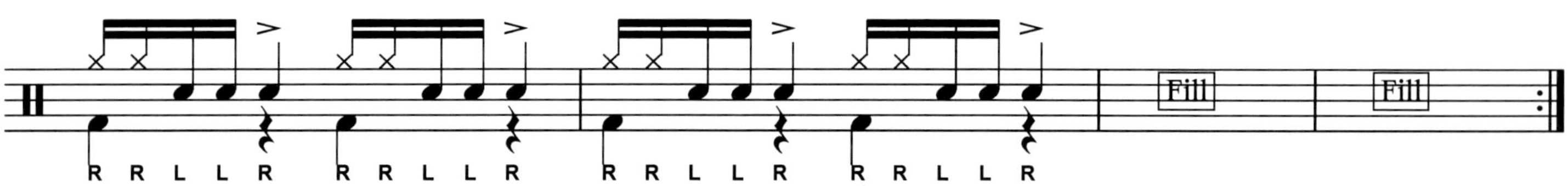

6 Stroke Roll

Snare Drum

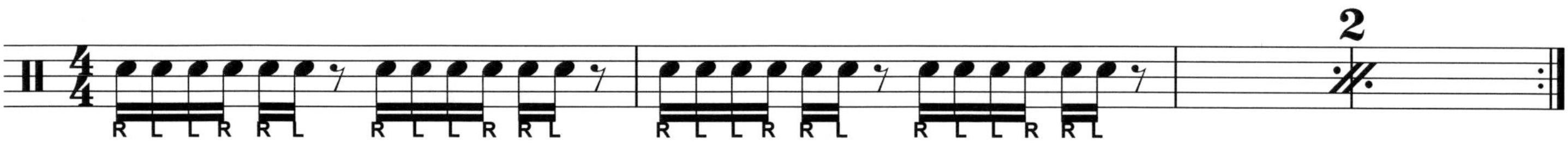

Groove

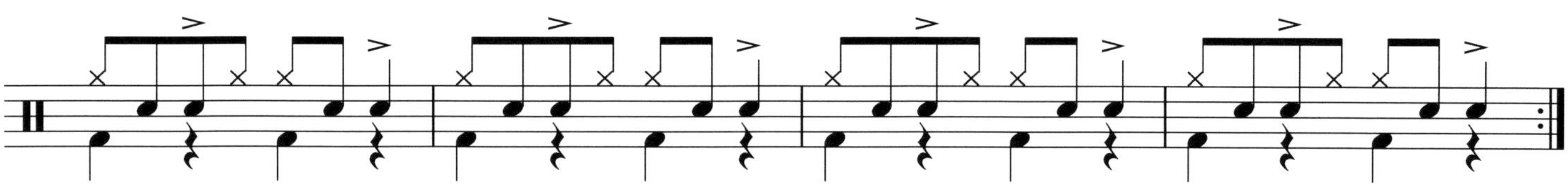

Play along to the music track "Aliens":

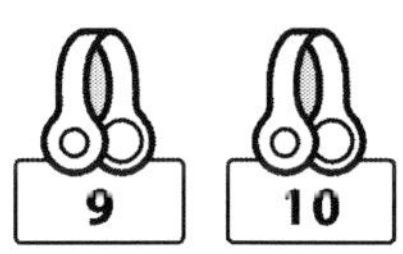

Fill

Open Fills

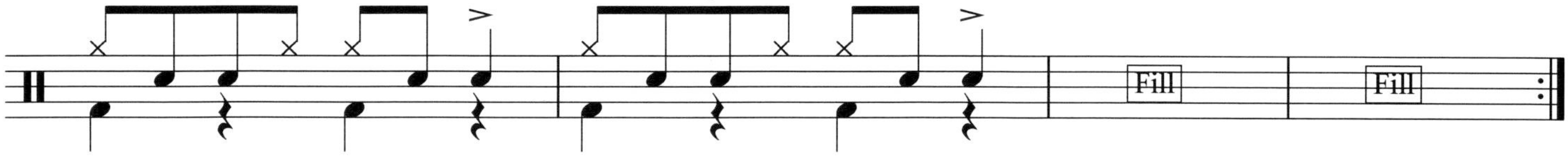

7 Stroke Roll

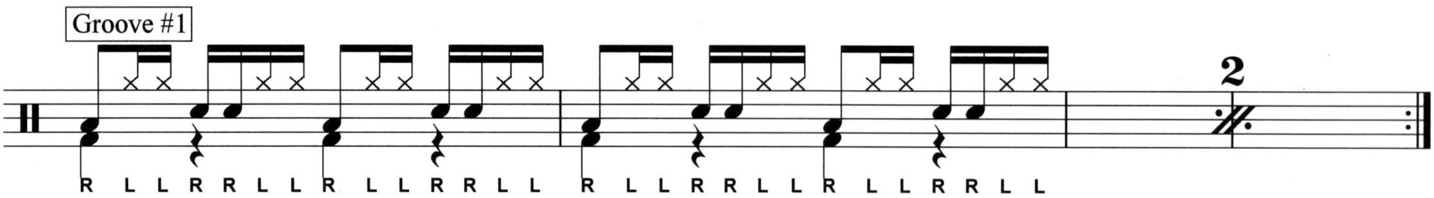

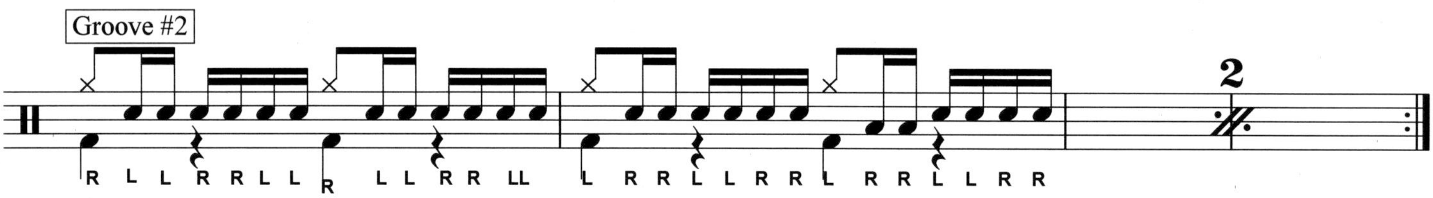

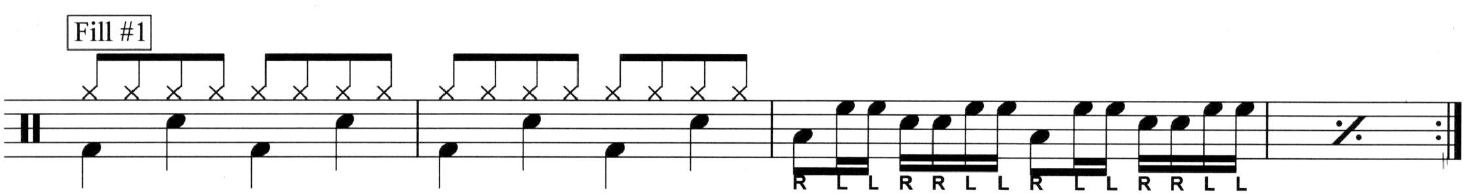

Play along to the music track "Aliens": 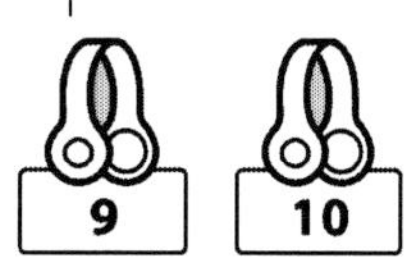

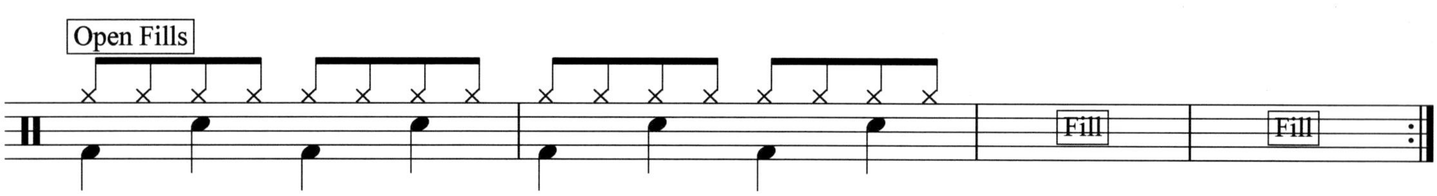

9 Stroke Roll

Snare Drum

Groove

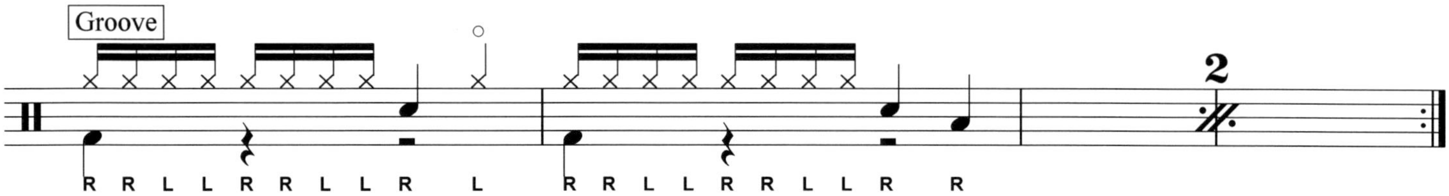

The circle above beat 4 refers to opening the hi-hat.

Fill

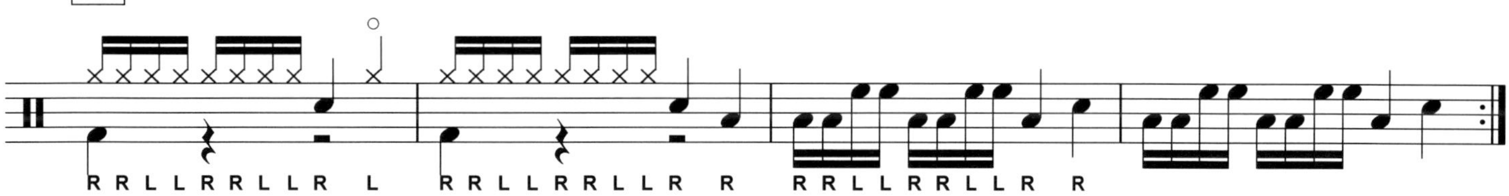

Play along to the music track "Half Time": 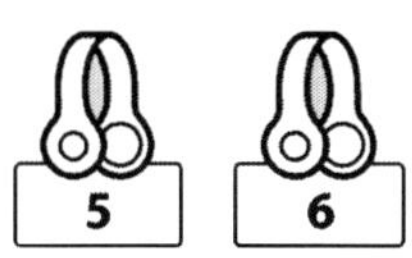

Open Fills

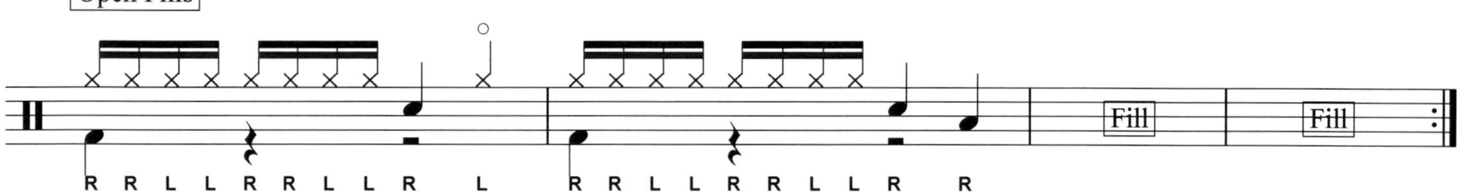

10 Stroke Roll

Snare Drum

Groove

Fill

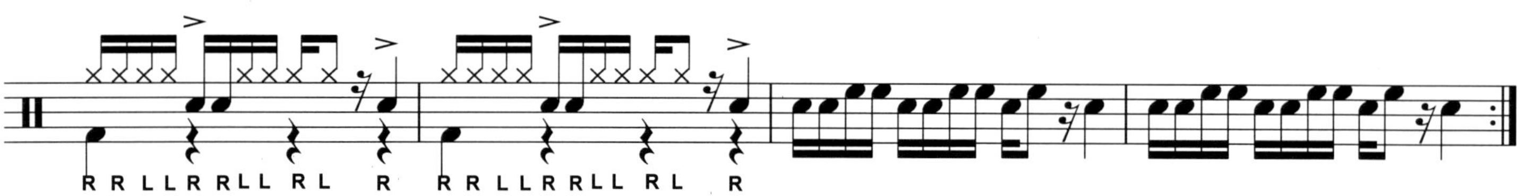

Play along to the music track "Funk":

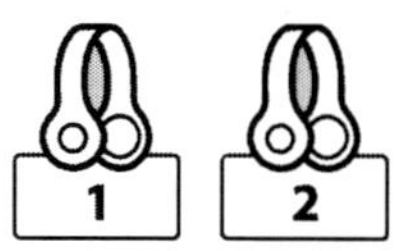

Open Fills

11 Stroke Roll

Snare Drum

Groove

Fill

Play along to the music track "Funk": 1 2 or "Aliens": 9 10

Open Fills

13 Stroke Roll

Snare Drum

Groove

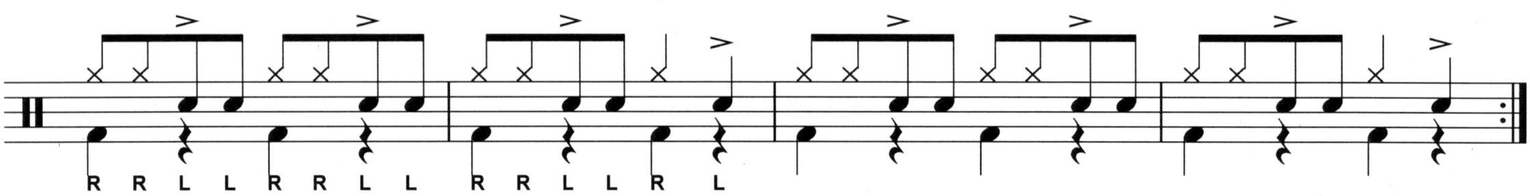

Play along to the music track "Aliens": 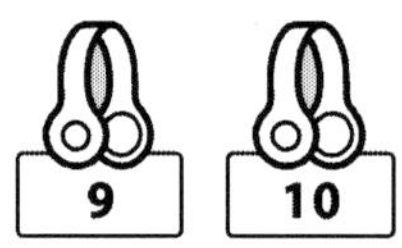

Fill

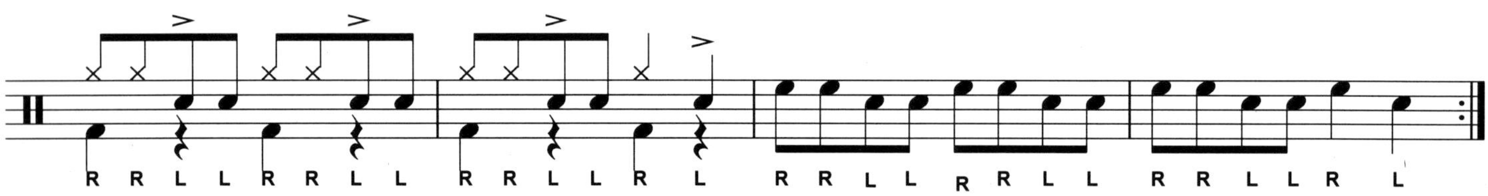

Open Fills

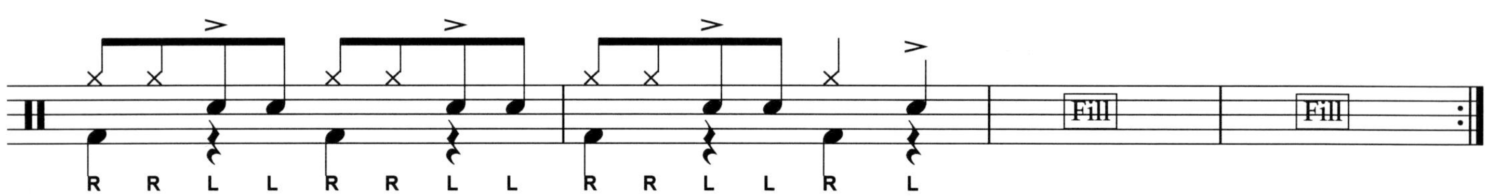

15 Stroke Roll

Snare Drum

Groove

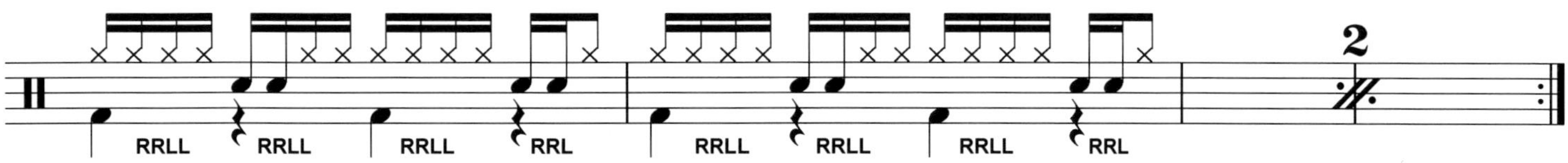

Fill

Play along with the music track "Aliens": 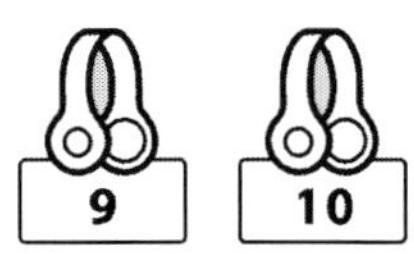

Open Fills

17 Stroke Roll

Snare Drum

Groove

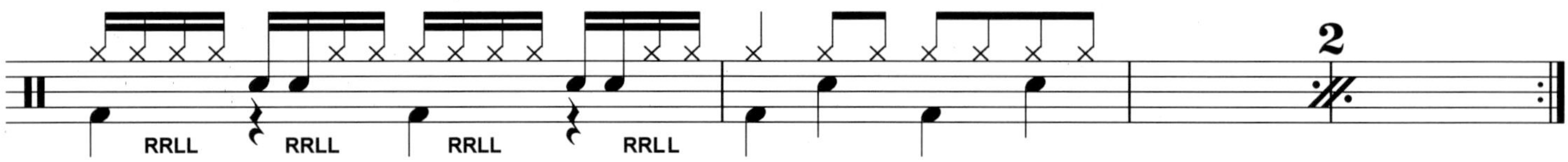

Fill

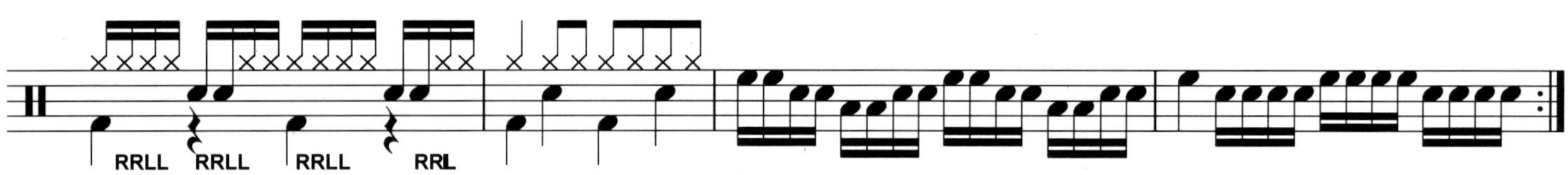

Play along to the music track "Funk": 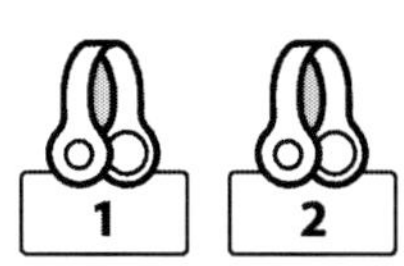

Groove

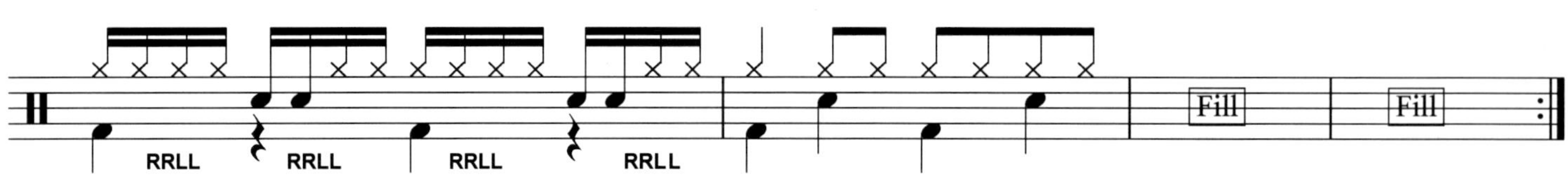

Paradiddles

Snare Drum

Groove

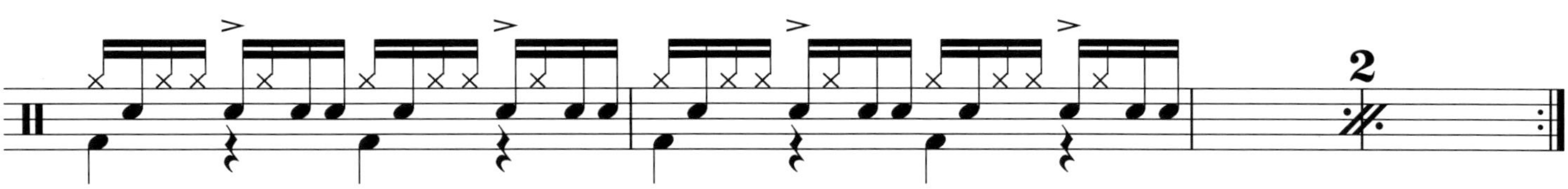

Play along with the music track "Funk": 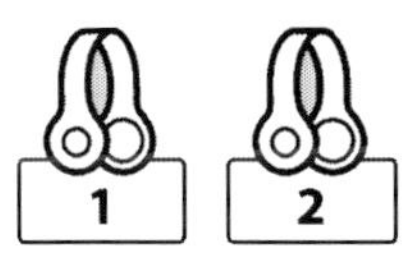

Fill

Open Fills

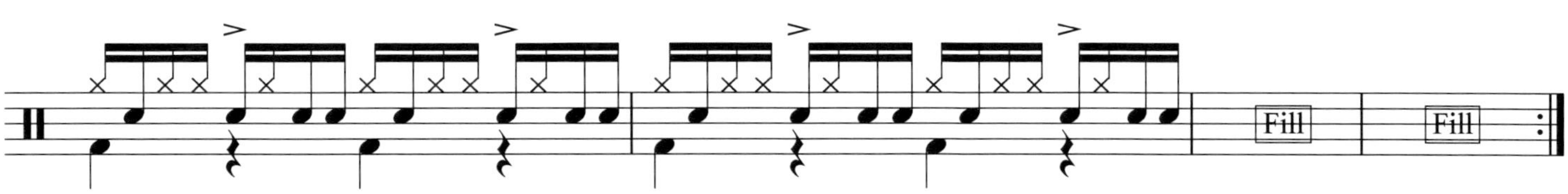

Double Paradiddle

Snare Drum

Groove

Play along to the track "Slow Blues":

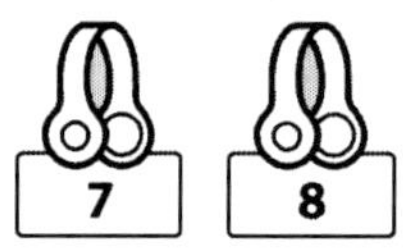

Fill

Open Fills

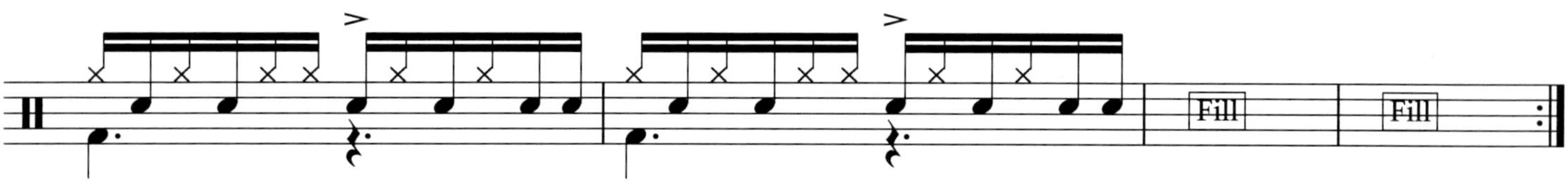

Triple Paradiddles

Snare Drum

Groove

Play along to the music track "Funk": 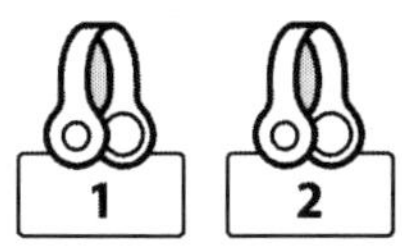

Fill

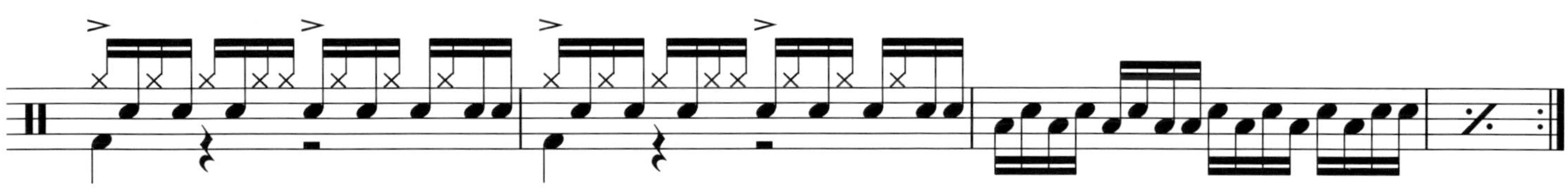

Open fills

Paradiddle - Diddle

Snare Drum

Groove

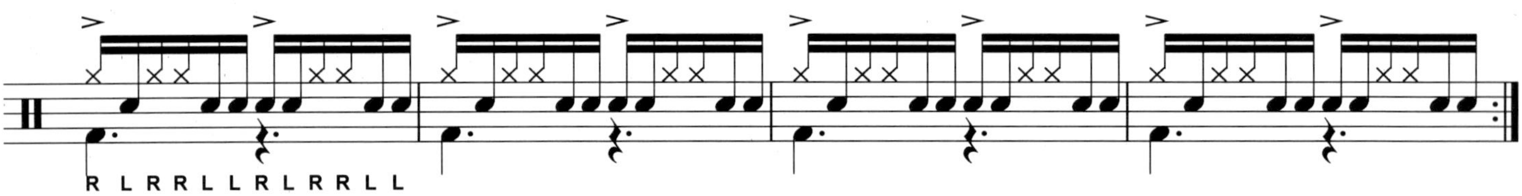

Fill

Play along to the music track "Slow Blues": 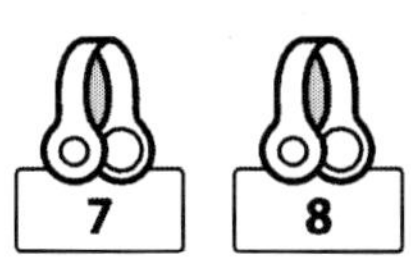

Open Fills

Flams

Snare Drum

Groove

Fills

Play along with the music track "Passport": 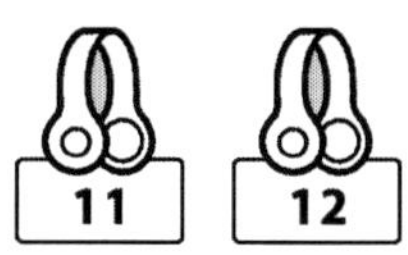

Open Fills

Flam Accent

Snare Drum

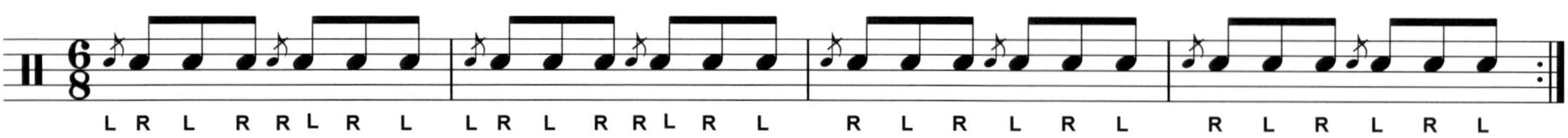

Groove

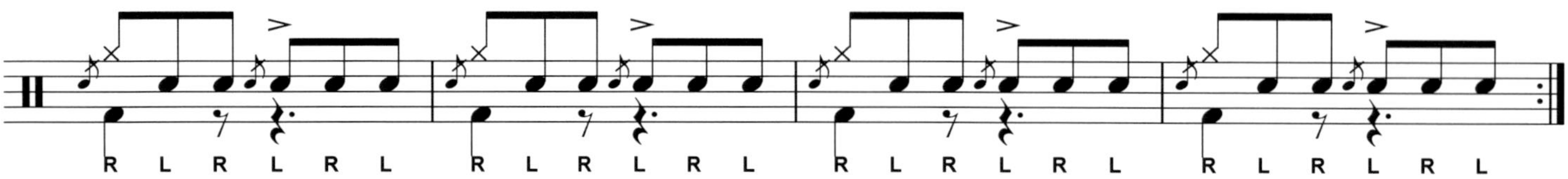

Fill

Play along with the track "Slow Blues": 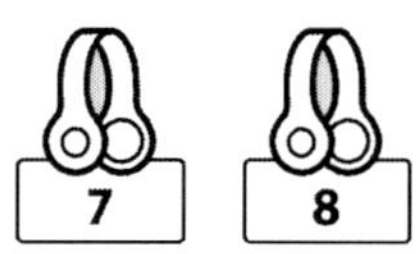

Fill #2

Open Fills

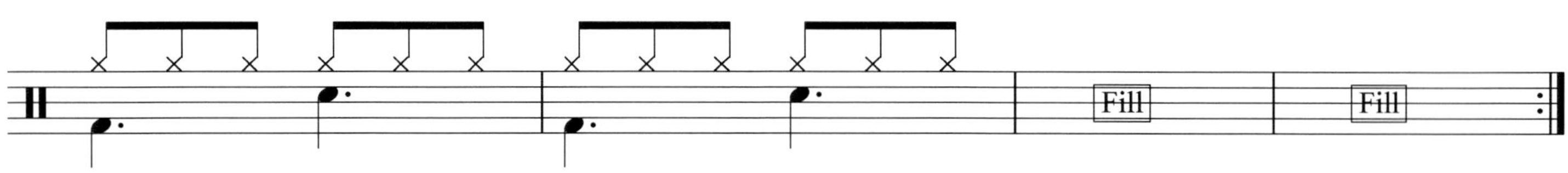

Flam Tap

Snare Drum

Now try the same Flam Tap sticking pattern in a different rhythm.

Snare Drum Shuffle

Play along with the music track "Gilbert": 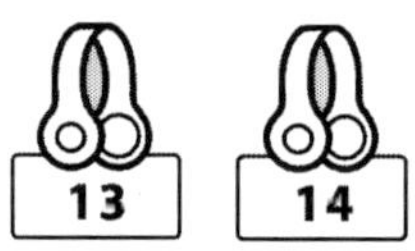

Fill

Open Fills

Flamacue

Snare Drum

Groove

Groove #2

Play along with the music track "Half Time": 5 6

Fills

Open Fills

Flam Paradiddle

Snare Drum

In the following exercises, the grace note of the Flam is played on a different surface.

Groove

Play along to the music track "Half Time": 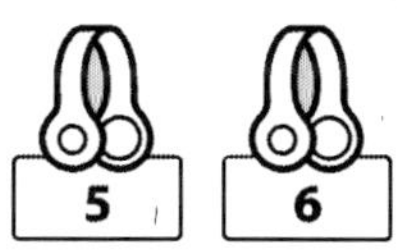

Fill

Open Fills

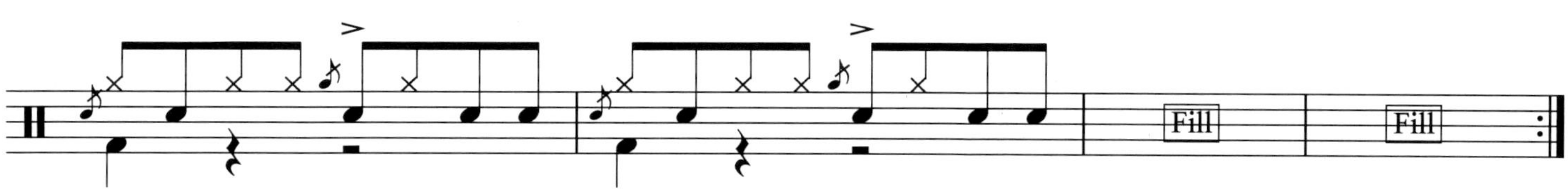

Flammed Mill

Snare Drum

Groove

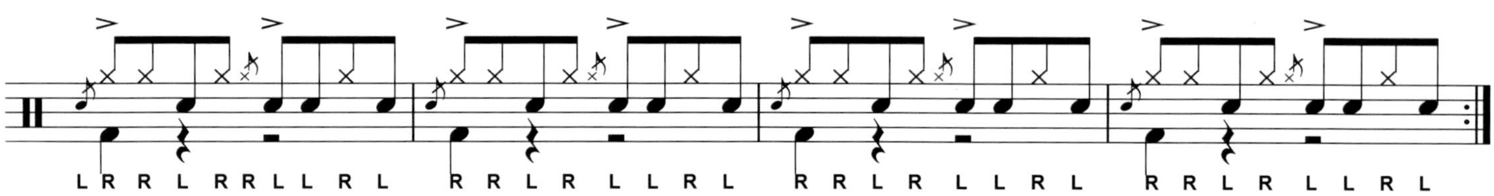

Fills

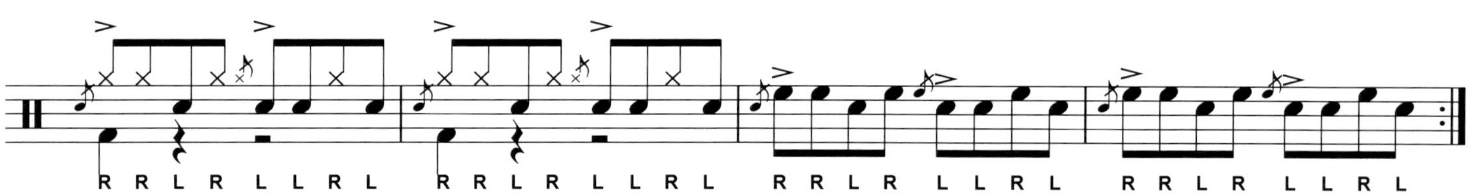

Play along to the music track "Half Time": 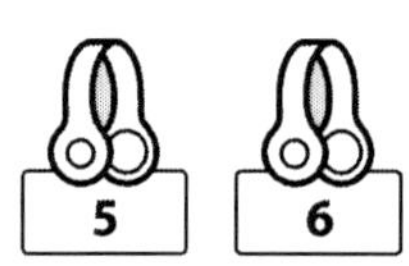

Open Fills

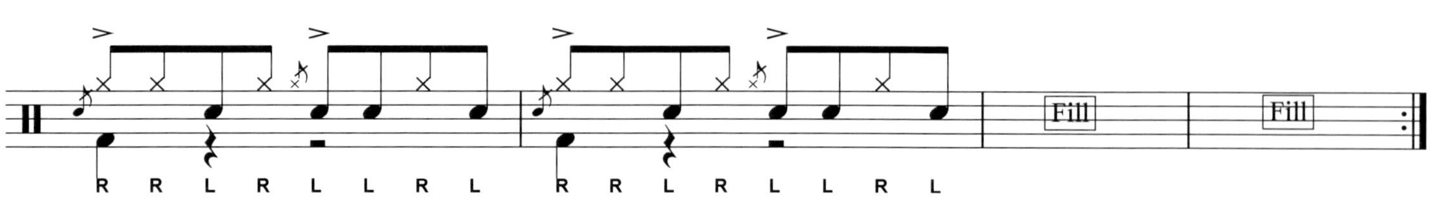

Flam Paradiddle-Diddle

Snare Drum

Groove

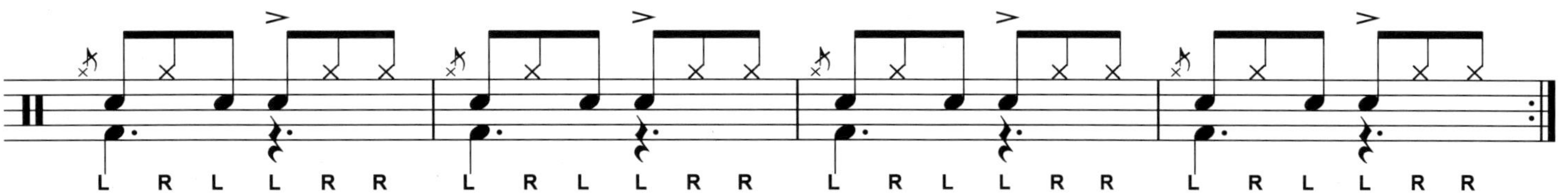

Play along with the music track "Slow Blues":

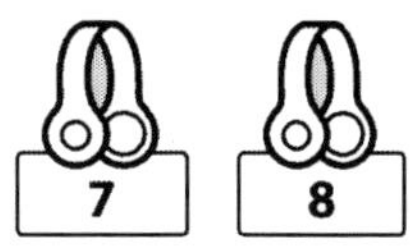

Fills

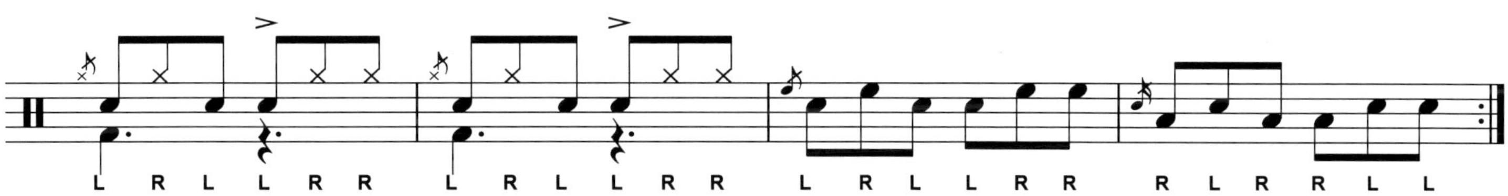

Open Fills

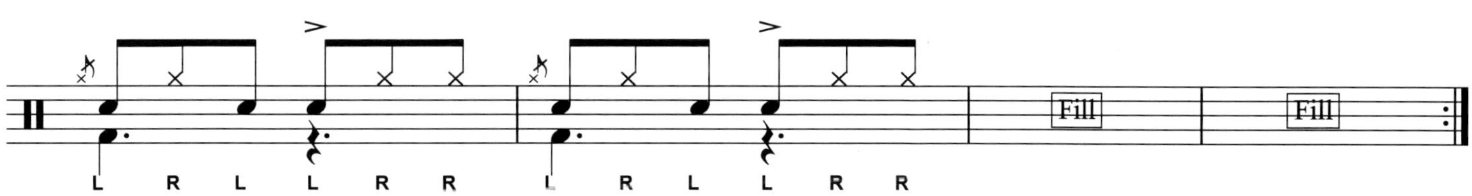

Pataflafla

Snare Drum

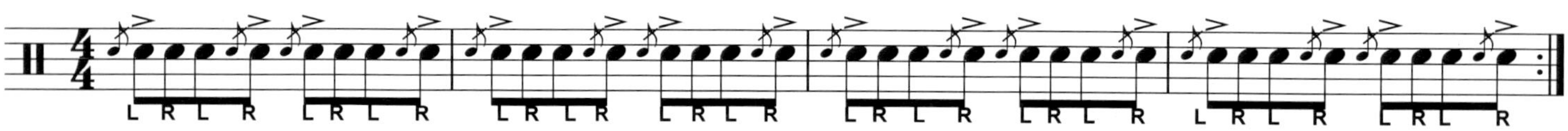

Groove

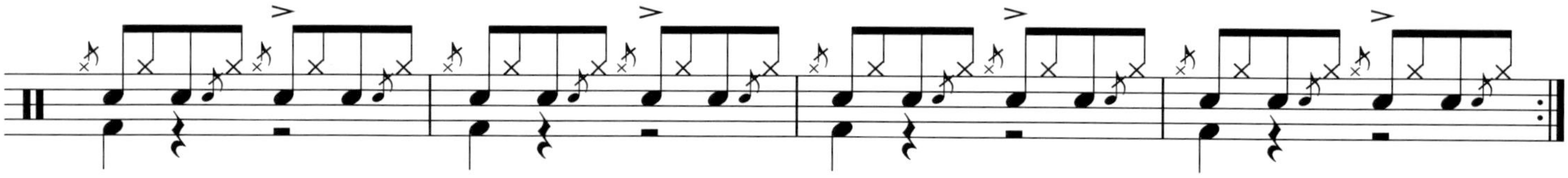

Play along with the music track "Half Time": 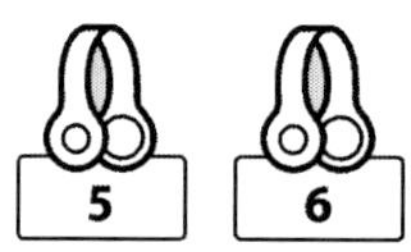

Fill

Open Fills

Swiss Army Triplets

Snare Drum

Groove

Play along to the music track "Slow Blues": 7 8

Fill

Open Fills

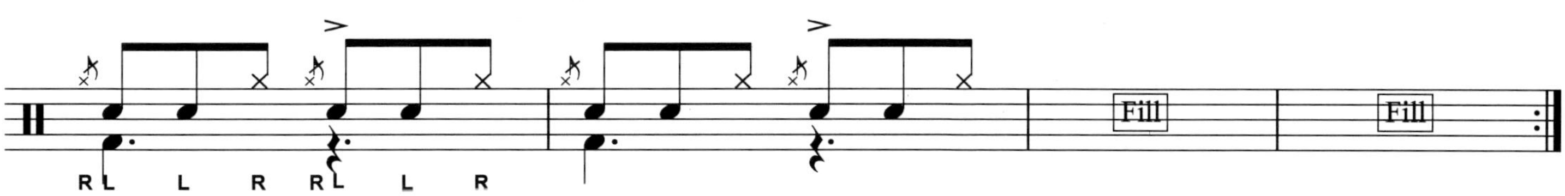

Inverted Flam Tap

Snare Drum

Now try the same Flam Tap pattern in a different rhythm:

Shuffle Groove

Play along with the music track "Gilbert": 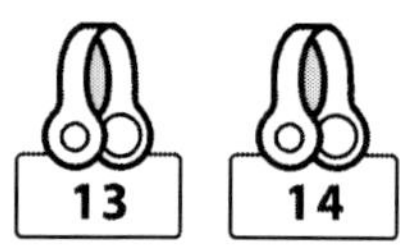

Fill

Open Fills

Flam Drag

Snare Drum

Groove

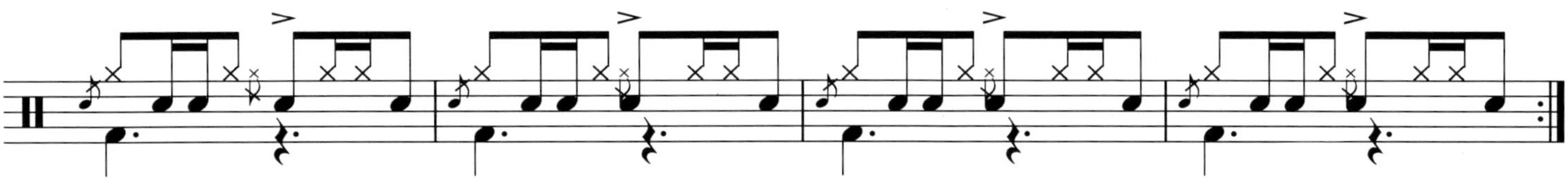

Play along with the track "Slow Blues": 7 8

Fill

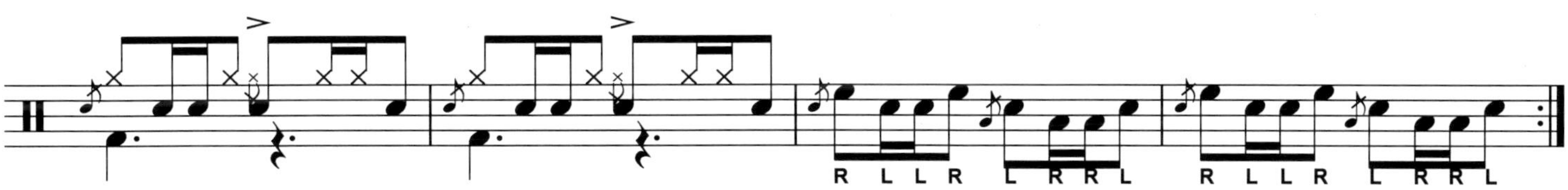

Open Fills

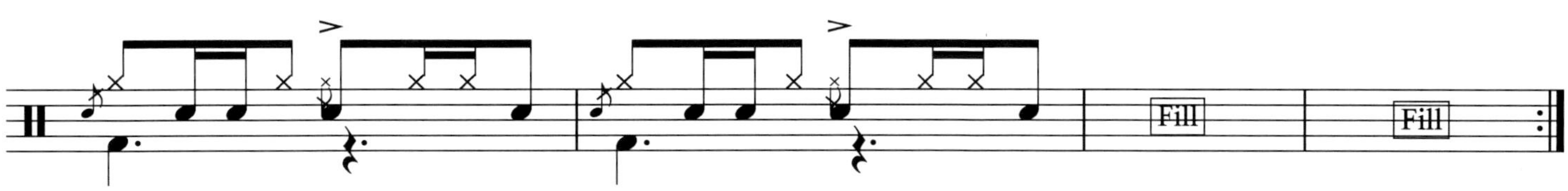

Drag

Snare Drum

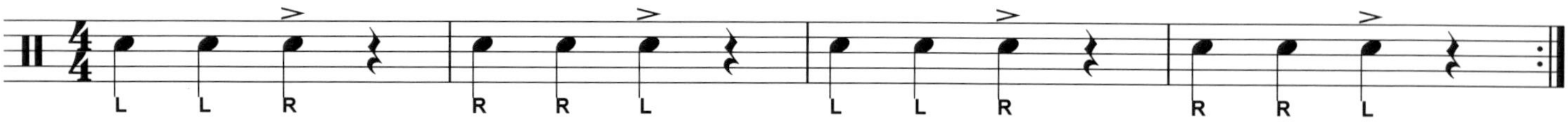

Groove

This excercise creates a "train" groove.

Groove #2

Here's another "train" groove.

Fill

Play along with the track "What a Drag": 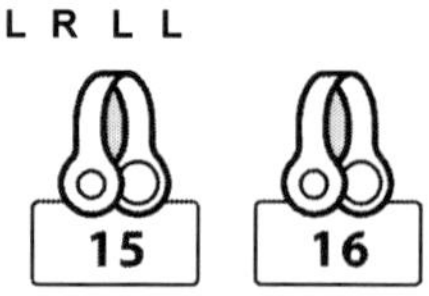

Open Fills

Drag Tap

Snare Drum

Groove

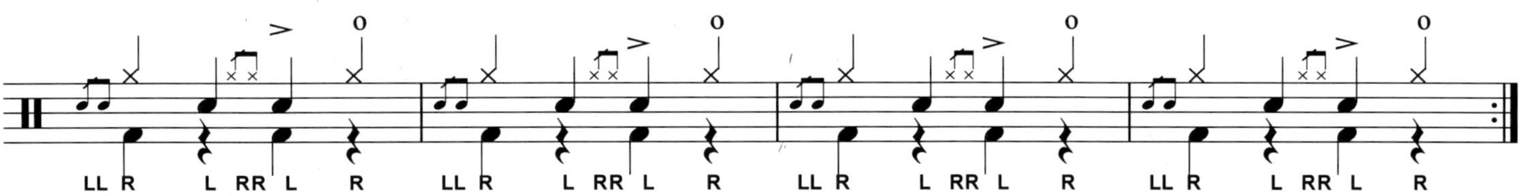

Fill

Play along to the music track "Half Time": 5 6

Open Fills

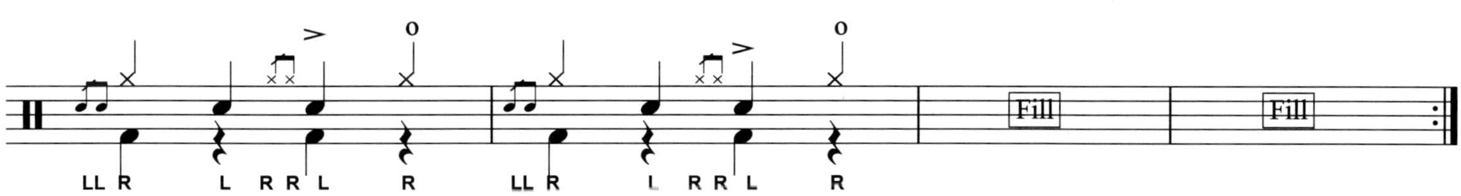

Double Drag Tap

Snare Drum

Groove

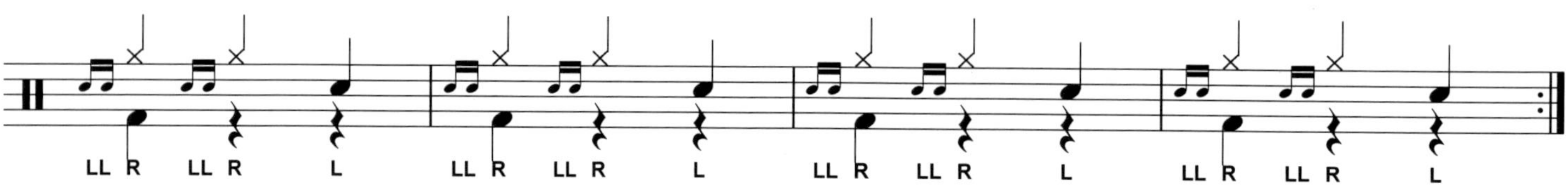

Fill

Play along to the track "Love Seat": 17 18

Open Fills

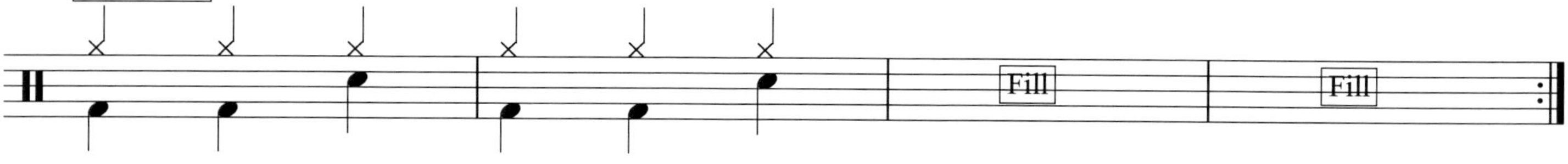

Lesson 25

Snare Drum

Play along to the music track "Gilbert": 13 14 or "What a Drag": 15 16

Shuffle Groove

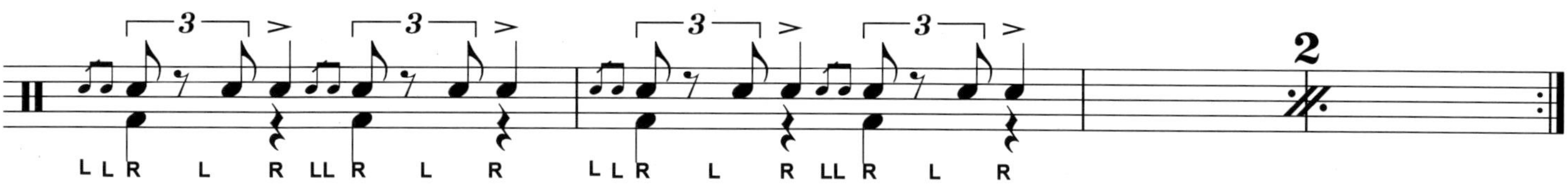

Fill

Open Fills

Single Dragadiddle

Snare Drum

Groove

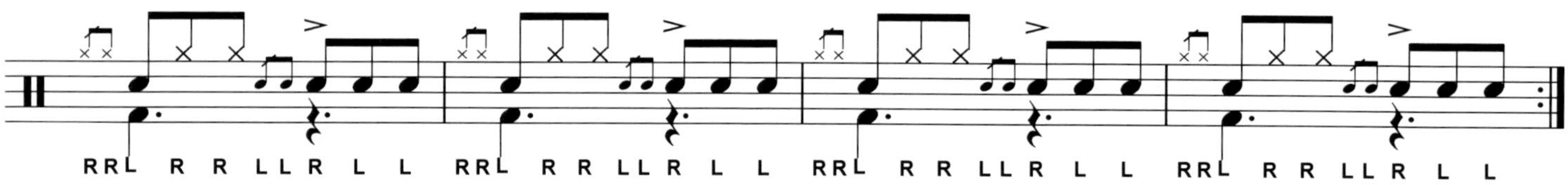

Play along to the music track "Slow Blues": 7 8

Fill

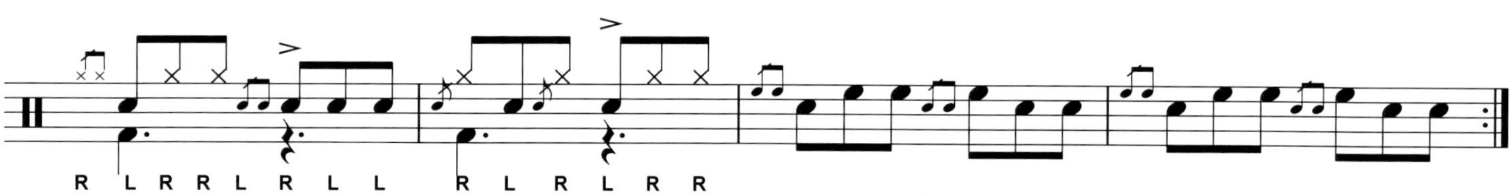

Open Fills

Drag Paradiddle

Snare Drum

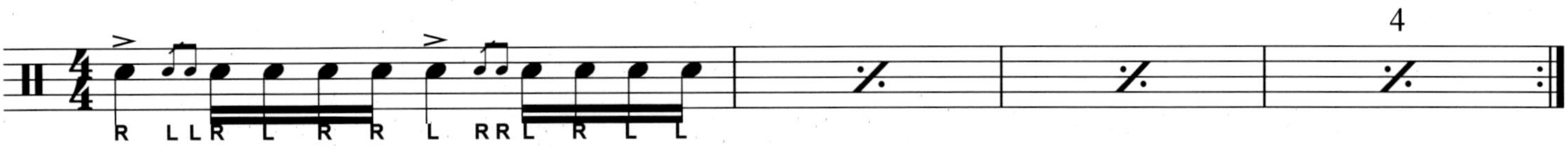

Groove

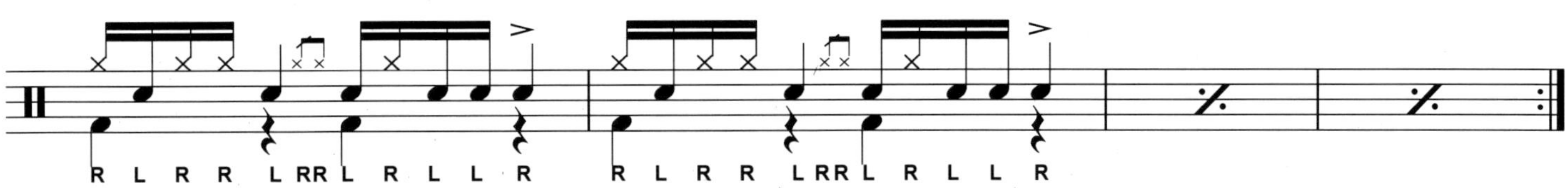

Play along to the music track "Funk": 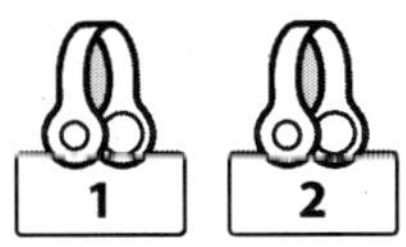

Fill

Open Fills

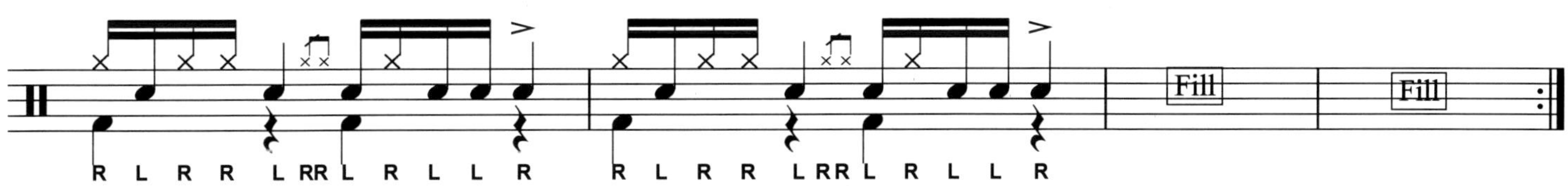

Drag Paradiddle #2

Snare Drum

Groove

Fill

Play along to the music track "Half Time": 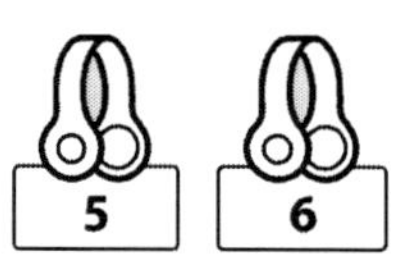

Open Fills

Ratamacue

Snare Drum

Groove

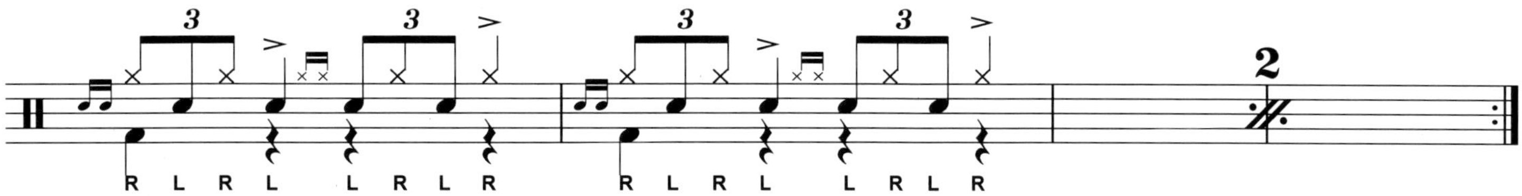

Fill

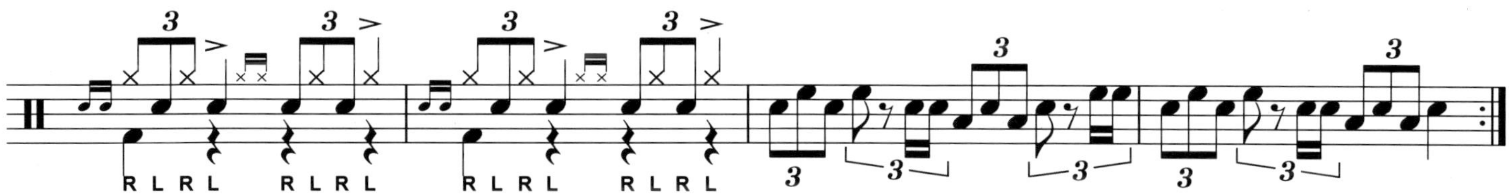

Play along to the music track "Backroads": 19 20 or "Buckshot": 3 4

Open Fills

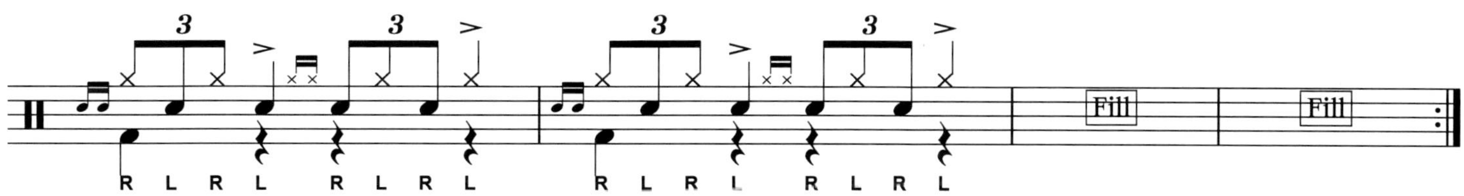

Double Ratamacue

Snare Drum

Groove

Fill

Play along to the music track "Love Seat": 17 18

Open Fill

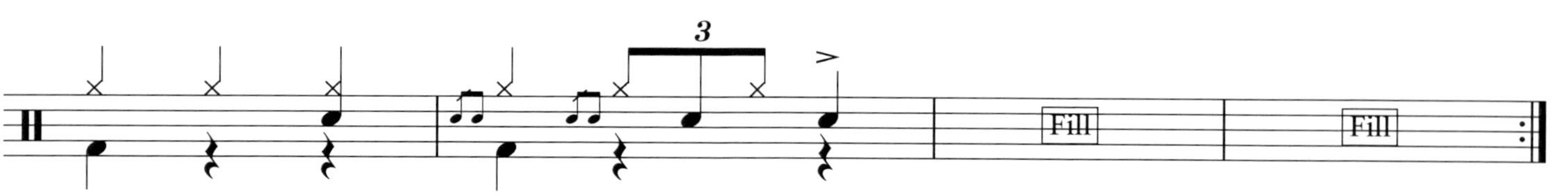

Triple Ratamacue

Snare Drum

Groove

Play along to the music track "Backroads": 19 20 or "Buckshot": 3 4

Fill

Open Fills

About the Author

Ron Wilson

Ron Wilson holds a Master of Music degree from William Paterson University and a Bachelor's Degree in Percussion Performance from the State University of New York at Purchase.

Ron's varied performing resume reflects his wide range of musical abilities. Ron has worked with accomplished artists such as Mitch Ryder, Darlene Love, Mick Jones, Mark Lindsay, Badfinger, Dee Dee Ramone, Gary US Bonds, Gloria Gaynor, the Vanilla Fudge, Sam Moore, Dion, Tavares, Tommy Roe, The Stylistics, Billy J. Kramer, The Miracles and jazz artists Dave Valentin, Lew Soloff, Lee Muziker, Darmon Meader, Rhonda Ross and the Guy Lombardo Band to name but a few. Ron is currently working as Musical Director for Lou Christie. Ron is also a published composer and author.

Ron has performed in such prestigious venues as Carnegie Hall, the Meadowlands Arena, the Apollo Theater, the Ed Sullivan Theater, Boston Symphony Hall, the Rock n' Roll Hall of Fame, Nassau Coliseum, Walt Disney World, New Jersey Performing Arts Center and countless other venues across the globe. You may have seen Ron performing on nationally broadcast television shows such as the CBS Early Show and PBS Concerts.

When not performing live, Ron keeps busy with recording sessions, teaching and composing.

For more information visit www.ronwilson.net.

Other Mel Bay Drum Books

24 Snare Drum Solos for Concerts, Recitals & Contests (Maroni)
Beyond Stick Control (Meyer)
Complete Music for Fife and Drum (Sweet)
Drum Rudiment Chart (Maroni)
Drum Rudiments (Maroni)
Drumstick Finger Systems and Techniques (Marucci)
Essential Snare Drum Exercises (Marucci)
Fantastic Hands (Fitch)
Fun with the Drums (Brophy)
Fundamentals of Rhythm for the Drummer (Maroni)
A Natural Development in Drumming Technique (Ciago)
A New Approach to Odd-Times for Drum Set (Lyman)
Basics of Drumming Wall Chart (Hofmann)
Complete Modern Drum Set (Briggs)
Crosstraining (Lewis)
Double Basics Complete Double Bass Drum (Vinciguerra)
Drum and Bass Synchronicity: The Ultimate Rhythm Section Workout (Prushko/Dozier)
Drum Fills: The Basics and Beyond (Williams)
Drum Set Tunes (Schinstine/Hoey)
Drumming Facts, Tips & Warm-Ups (Marucci)
Drumstick Finger Systems and Techniques (Marucci)
Extreme Drumset Solos for Recitals, Contests and Fun (Leyman)
Fantastic Feet: Stepping Outside the Box (Fitch)
Fill Workbook (Richardson)
Hot Drum Grooves Made Easy/Large Print Edition (Morton)
Intro to Polyrhythms (Ari Hoenig/Weidenmueller)
Killer Fillers (Morton)
Killer Technique: Drumset (Green)
Learn to Burn: Drum Set (Perlson)
Mel Bay's Best Drumset Manuscript Book
Metric Modulations: Contracting & Expanding Time Within Form (Ari Hoenig/Weidenmueller)
Musical Drumset Solos for Recitals, Contests and Fun (Leyman)
Ostinatos for the Melodic Drumset (Leytham)
Paradiddles Redefined for Drum Set (Vega)
Rhythmic Aerobics (Ryan)
Rhythmic Aerobics Volume 2 (Ryan)
Secrets of the Greats: Drumset Exercises for a Professional Sound (Silverman)
Studies in Drumset Independence Vol. 1 (Vinciguerra)
Studies in Drumset Independence Vol. 2 (Vinciguerra)

WWW.MELBAY.COM

Other Mel Bay Drum Books